DISCARD

```
PS          Stryk, Dan,
3569          1951-
.T75
L5          Lives.
1990
```

$14.95

LIVES

Other Books by Dan Stryk

TO MAKE A LIFE (Poems)
THE ARTIST AND THE CROW (Poems)

LIVES

Dan Stryk

Mellen Poetry Series
Volume 6

The Edwin Mellen Press
Lewiston•Queenston
Lampeter

Library of Congress Cataloging-in-Publication Data

Stryk, Dan, 1951-
    Lives / Dan Stryk.
      p. cm. -- (Mellen poetry series ; v. 6)
    ISBN 0-88946-890-7
    I. Title. II. Series.
    PS3569.T75L5 1990
    811'.54--dc20
                                                        90-36261
                                                               CIP

This is volume 6 in the continuing series
Mellen Poetry Series
Volume 6 ISBN 0-88946-890-7
MPS Series ISBN 0-88946-885-0

Edited by Patricia Schultz
A CIP catalog record for this book
is available from the British Library.

Copyright © 1990 Dan Stryk
All rights reserved. For information contact:
                    The Edwin Mellen Press

Box 450   Box 67
Lewiston, New York   Queenston, Ontario
USA 14092   CANADA L0S 1L0
                    The Edwin Mellen Press, Ltd.
                      Lampeter, Dyfed, Wales
                UNITED KINGDOM SA48 7DY

              Printed in the United States of America

For Leslie

And to the living memory
of Lucy and my grandmothers

CONTENTS

TALES FROM A MIDWEST FARM 1

    Winds of the Midwest 3
    Swelter.. 4
    Confessions of a Black Sheep on a Farm 5
    Hollyhocks 7
    Parable 8
    Watering the Herd 9
    Nighttrain 10
    'Unfinished' Symphony 11
    Vacancies 13
    They Will Stay 15
    Away From Things 16
    The Ice-Bound Months 16
    Six Images of the Farm Turning to Spring 17

CHRYSALIS 19

    Chrysalis 21
    Poppies 23
    Redwings, Again 24
    Luna Moth 27
    The Geranium 29
    Fishing After Rain 30
    Nutgatherers 33
    Swallow Evening 34
    Winter Feeder by the Window, First of Dawn 35
    Beavers in Snow 37
    Life in Death 41
    Still Life 42

HUMAN NATURE ... 43

- Bats ... 45
- The Beautiful Face ... 47
- On Taking My Old Father to the Chicago Aquarium ... 49
- Antique ... 50
- Saints of Spring ... 51
- Porch ... 52
- The Sad and Noble Poems of the Ancient Chinese Concubines ... 53
- Lynn ... 54
- Smoke ... 55
- Cave Bull ... 57
- Lemonade Stand ... 58
- Push-Mower ... 58
- Beginners' Luck ... 59
- Squirrel Electrocuted on the Power Line ... 60
- The Skunk ... 60
- Poison Ivy ... 62

ACKNOWLEDGMENTS

Grateful acknowledgment is made to the following publications in which many of these poems first appeared: *Aldebaran, Beloit Poetry Journal, Chariton Review, Commonweal, Confrontation, Hollins Critic, Kansas Quarterly, Mississippi Review, New Mexico Humanities Review, Paintbrush, Poetry Miscellany, Poetry Northwest, Quarterly West, Snowy Egret, Southern Humanities Review, Southern Poetry Review, Southwest Review, Sow's Ear, Spectrum, TriQuarterly, Western Humanities Review, Wisconsin Review.*

"Swelter" was anthologized in *Writers Forum 6* (University of Colorado), and appeared as part of a longer sequence in the full-length collection *The Artist and the Crow*, Purdue University Press, 1984.

"Vacancies" was anthologized in *Poems: Prairie Style, Sixteen DeKalb Area Poets*, DeKalb Arts Commission, DeKalb, Illinois.

A selection of these poems, some in earlier forms, first appeared in the limited-edition chapbook *To Make a Life*, Confluence Press (Lewis-Clark State College).

Portions of this book were written with the support of a National Endowment for the Arts Poetry Fellowship, for which I am grateful to the Endowment.

Work on this book was aided by an Artists Grant from the Illinois Arts Council.

TALES FROM A MIDWEST FARM

Without a jot of ambition left
I let my nature flow where it will.
There are ten days of rice in my bag
And, by the hearth, a bundle of firewood.
Who prattles of illusion or nirvana?
Forgetting the equal dusts of name and fortune,
Listening to the night rain on the roof of my hut,
I sit at ease, both legs stretched out.

—Ryokan (1757-1831), Zen monk

WINDS OF THE MIDWEST

The field's mane swishes . . .

swallows   circling far above
    toss
             into the blunt white jaws
   of clouddrift;

everywhere wind flows,
   rustling in the lank elm stand,
whipping in the tassels of the corn,—
   everywhere,
            yet everywhere   flows separately.

The rippling palomino of the field
                   gallops
   the loam prairie on its glacial hooves,
round mastiff-lair of grainshed,
bloodred shrine of barn. . . .

SWELTER

The heat has filled the trees
& frizzled dandelion heads,
the cattle salivate & bunch
dank-furred inside the shed.
And everywhere the dung smell's
solid as a living thing,
& solid as another swarm the flies.
Drenched, we drudge the morning
patching screens, & still
the mad buzz & the midday darkening.
(The bigger take to pastureland
to clog the horses' eyes.)

Dead heat on the summer farm
has hatched a wild life-lust in the air,
that seems, at once, too thin.
All's gone to sweat!—
the smell of our own bodies, cramped
within these teeming walls,
has wound about us like a caul.

* * *

A horsefly,
slowly squeezing through warped frame,
falls to spin its death-buzz on the rug.

CONFESSIONS OF A BLACK SHEEP ON A FARM

    It is quiet, early morning,
    wife at work; I lie back
    in an armchair, book, unreading.
    Instantly the window comes alive
    with sparrows hovering all awhirr
    like bees. Their chatter rising,
        furious,
    they've come to nest sagged rafters
    once again. And once again
    my tan house cat leaps to the ledge
    & rises, paws on window, ears pricked up:—
    the clicking, ravenous sounds of spring
    escaping from her throat.
    Why do I write down these things,
    years already dun upon my scalp?
    Seldom have I tried, in truth,
    to scale much higher than the rafters
    slumped above our moss-grown porch,
        than the barn loft at the farm on which we live.

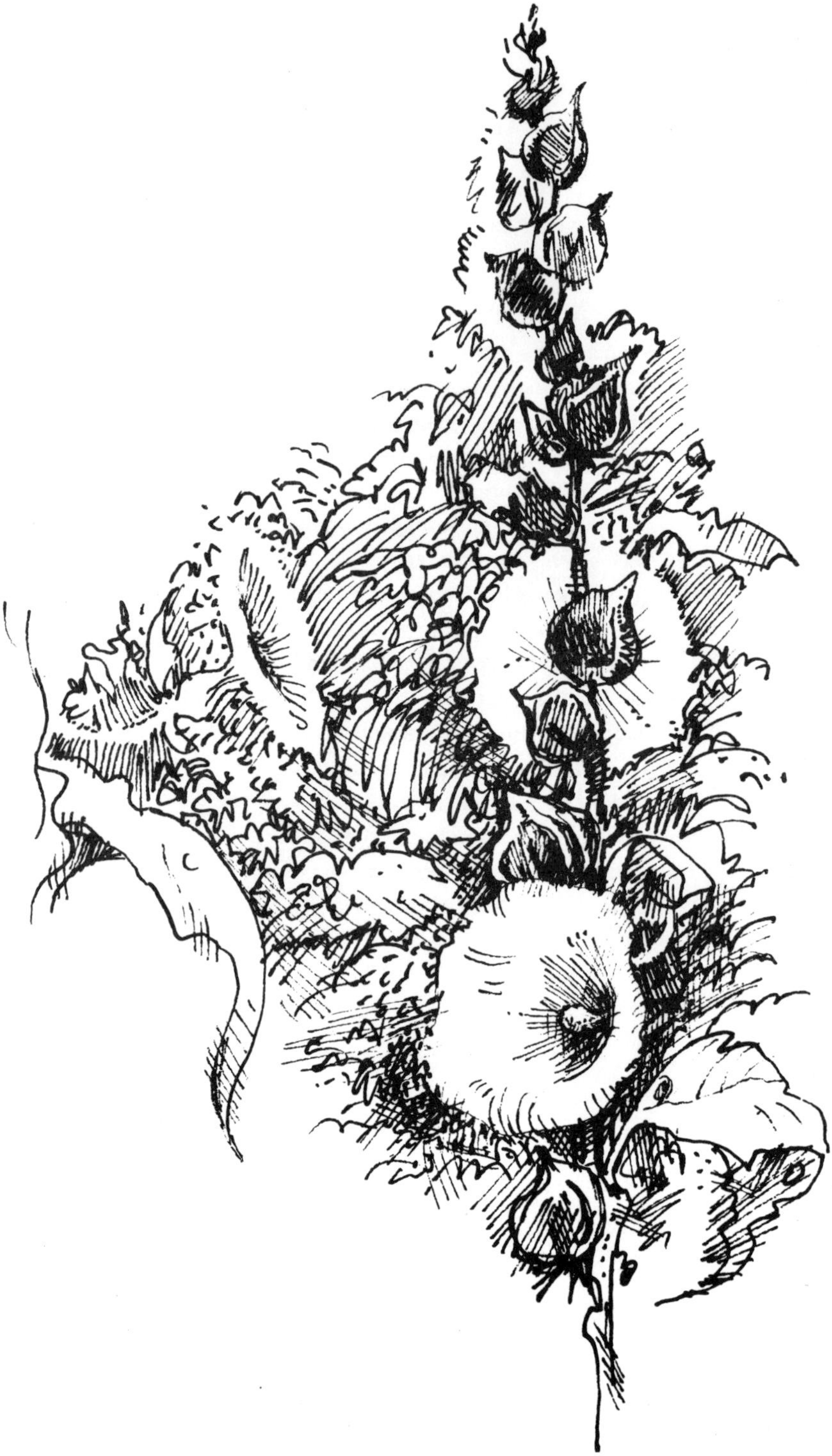

HOLLYHOCKS

Lank mendicants, they spring
   each year, a soft surprise,
to balance long days, dim or bright,
   moist blooms raised like

bowls of light—faint glow in cloud,
   brimmed full in sun—
long budded necks outstretched
   against the telephone pole's

mute grey & the scarred
   wall of the garage. A balance
firm: bald ugly nodes
   coarse, dry & often stained

with rust, but still
   the limpid lake-smooth
flowers interspersed
   on other nodes, like chance—

their ragged glowing
   stem. Then battered down
in cloudburst, pounded flat
   beneath the crooked hoop

on the garage, the rage
   of daylit boys, until
their long necks line
   the guillotine of night—

swept heat-flash, lancing
   rain—yet in the morning
partially rise up again,
   all summer long, these Chinese

sages, just enough. Clean spare robes
   of salmon, white, soft-fluttering,
their upraised bowls,
   a few new blooms . . .

PARABLE

Living is an art; and, to practice it well, men need not only acquired skill but also a native tact and taste.
—Aldous Huxley

The great beige bull
    lies still
   beneath the apple tree.
I rev the engine,
   hoping that he'll rise.
     He does not budge.
I prod him with a pebble,
   snapping off
     his deep-thewed side.
   And still he chews,
    oblivious,
    dewlap waving in stiff breeze.
Inside,
  I floor the motor,
    let it roar:
he merely shifts his eyes,
   then shifts them back
    like muddy hollows
   toward the swell of summer hills.
Spinning down slope-gravel,
  milling dust,
   I glance into the mirror,
    start to laugh:
The great beige bull
   has risen
   like a quaking sandstone bluff
to follow a small farmcat through the grass.

WATERING THE HERD

Faucet squeals,
breaks muddy
through black hose.—
Long dark tongues
    writhe up
to lap the tip;
    I plunge
the nozzle down
to free the jet.

The herd now lowers
tough-furred heads,
    dehorned,
into the burbling trough.
There is delight
of kind, it seems,
in swilling closeness
of their brawn.

I now turn back,
    unseen,
toward the barn.

NIGHTTRAIN

Wind ticking the shriveled husks,
we near the autumn field,

your hand in mine. Nightfall
quickens, ghostly wave of stalks

bends distant lights. A whistle
spurs the nightbreeze, startles us

once more, out of ourselves.
The northbound rumbles slowly

over the railbed's weathered
ties. Lights pool down the ballast

trail: our cannery's new stock
of Southern tin: the hillbred migrants'

livelihood and dirge. We sense
their restive sleep in roughboard

barracks by the plant. The whistle
blows again. Two watchmen, antlike,

lift the chute, wait its spotlit
disgorge to the night. The trainlights

dim. Black engine crackles faintly
in the dock. We turn to walk

the southfield home. The corn's
been picked, the dry field gathering

the sleep of dust. Those withered
autumn husks of Illinois.

'UNFINISHED' SYMPHONY

I draw back. The candle gutters
in the slight breeze through the window
I leave open just a crack, warm nights
& cool. This slight link, suspiration

of the outside world, I would yet
feel. My wife & son's long breaths
well up from deep in other rooms.
As always now, so near & far.

But tonight I sense day's vegetables
they've planted down below,
the play of light on sunflowers'
enormous fallen heads, tomato vines

translucent now & slanting in their
death-colors of fall, crisp rhythms
of brown witherings that rattle
all night long in waves

of breeze. In silences between,
I try to watch them *closely*—beam
the play of light with my still
mind. But it remains dark, dark,

against the lead-black pane, only
a glint of candlelight on tape
that holds the jagged mountain range
of a long crack I've pondered years

& often trekked with fingers guided
by night-heavy eyes. The notes
to end it all, to let all journeys
cease at last, are there, I sense,

just beyond the mountains & the glass,
as near as my own fluttering
breath, just beyond the window's
opaque slab. But the more I gaze

into the night, to pierce & still resolve
the thing I am in clear pure
sound, my hand (faint traveler)
draws back in, dark, dark,

withholds the notes that would,
or not, complete me.

VACANCIES

The stubblefield lies snow-furrowed.
Dry stalks ringed with prints
of animals:—

here, a brush-hare's three-pronged
leap; there, a fieldmouse,
tentative,

had hopped a cornstalk
three times round,
and stopped

to sink, small haunch-prints
like a potter's flaw
among

the dainty hieroglyphs of
claws. All vacancies.
Our nostrils

burn, steam signals to the animals—
Beware! There's not a rustle
or a stir

in all the wild expanse of these prints.—
We're locked into a vacancy
of tiny inert things,

about to scatter the still air
in breath of dry brown
leaves!

The distant farmhouse greys
on the horizon. Dusk
fills, blue,

the vacancies of prints....
We suddenly awaken
to the grip

of flesh and blood, lift stiff feet,
again, toward the night-bulb
of the farm....

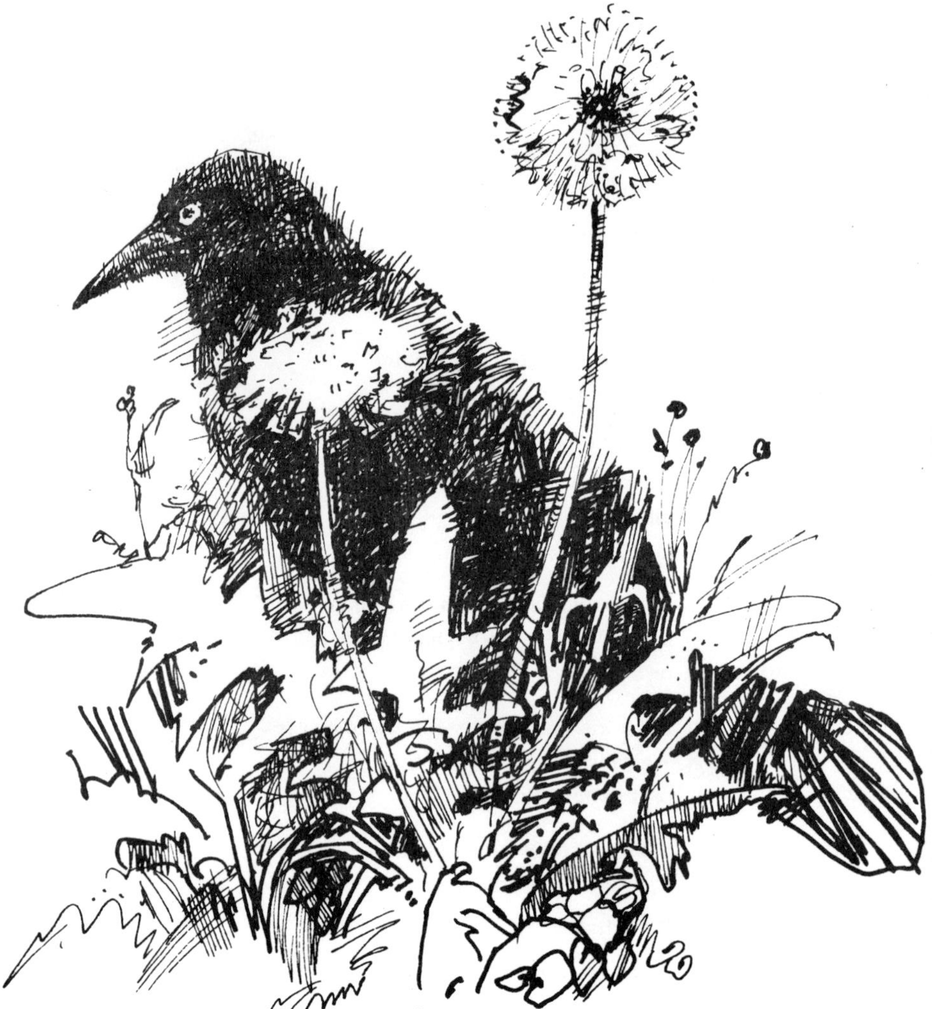

THEY WILL STAY

June squall. In morning's
   dandelion-light, the grackles,

starlings muscling each other
   by the worm-holes on our

wet, rank lawn. Breakfasting
   on the trellised porch, my wife

regrets the absence of the
   grosbeak's flashing breast

of rose—summer's lovely
   visitant of a few days, in certain

light a ruby flickering
   along the garden's border growth

of bolted-lettuce pagodas, squash vines,
   the purple flower of the pea,

a flickering like a small
   heart, now gone. While also missing

its small grace, my secret thought's
   how I love "grackle-light,"

those bobbing blue-green heads
   a luminous opposite of dandelion-

glow, a luminous harmony
   of opposites, like counterpoint,

Midwestern Bach, I start
   to laugh, to praise the truest

punctuation of our lawn's
   rank green, where they stalk

at home among the deadly nightshade
   petals left to trail decaying

stumps, sending off—like poems
   launched—the dandelions' spume.

AWAY FROM THINGS

Dawn a clotted bog, I sit inert.
Huddled in the mud hole

of my flesh. The tan cat
bounds the dimlit room, mad circle,

wily tail. Stalked lynx, she leaps
the armchair's back, claws snagged

to ragged top, slashed curse
of her ringed tail from upthrust tufts.

Outside, the morning's scarlet tints
bleed through the weed-tree's

fronds. A scent of lilac, vivid,
fills the air. I let her out.

Any moment she may roll herself
into the lengthy grass, sprout lambent

as forsythia
from soundless waves of green.

THE ICE-BOUND MONTHS

There were days we thought
the rafters would not stand
the white heat of our wrath,
and then the days we knew
we'd grown much firmer. Still,
winter locks scarred horns, and now
an old dead soberness
has stiffened
in the hawthorns' chill grey skins.

Below
the gutters' burnished snarl,
the clay hill grouts our farmhouse
to its bed.
The glazed earth will be turned again;
we must root deep
and wait,
sow our bitten spirits
to break flame in tawny wheat.

SIX IMAGES OF THE FARM
TURNING TO SPRING

1

Seedling dandelions strew rank grass.
The farmcat bellycrawls on butterfly
Which flutters yellow zigzags
Through the weeds.
I've given up the mower for the year.

2

Half-plowed, the furrows stretch
Beyond the tractor's mulching rig.
Dawn's violet dust has clogged my eyes.
There's much undone today,
But I am eager and alert:
My metal claws will turn the very land.

3

In three days what were leaflets
Have grown full and dark and crisp.
The cattle now regain a wild stealth,
Hide from us like deer
Among the leaves.

4

Today the starling hovers
Flailing wings,
Screams down at hissing cat
Through window-glass.
Her young peep from the rafters,
Necks craned thin,—
Oblivious to a mother's fury,
To a cat's knifed claws and mutterings.

5
There's a thin stream running east
Once river-wide
Till the silt slid from the hills
Where trees were axed
Or lost in blight.
Still, bending close
We see the algae eel
From silt-browned rocks,
The striders skip, slight ripple,
Skip;
Quick minnows whip clear bodies
From the rocks.

6
All's clear
And ringing cricket-crisp tonight,
Tremoring in warm soft breeze.
The night sky blooms
With distant lights.
Stopped on the turned earth
I hear them all.

CHRYSALIS

Whenever I catch a frog's eye . . . I stand quite still and try not to move or lift a hand since it would only frighten him. And standing thus it finally comes to me that this is the most enormous extension of vision of which life is capable: the projection of itself into other lives. This is the lonely, magnificent power of humanity. It is, far more than any spatial adventure, the supreme epitome of the reaching out.

—Loren Eiseley, *The Immense Journey*

CHRYSALIS

Mid-August we'd awakened
 to a radiance, but not
  the outthrust blue we sought

in the barren morning-glory's
 silent nest of heart-shaped
  green. Milkier than the leaf

it dangled from, by one
 thin pliant strand, pale-
  gold beads edged ridges

of its lantern-case
 of jade, like hammered
  distillations of the dew

and light, reflectors
 of the early-risen sun.
  Moisture from the morning

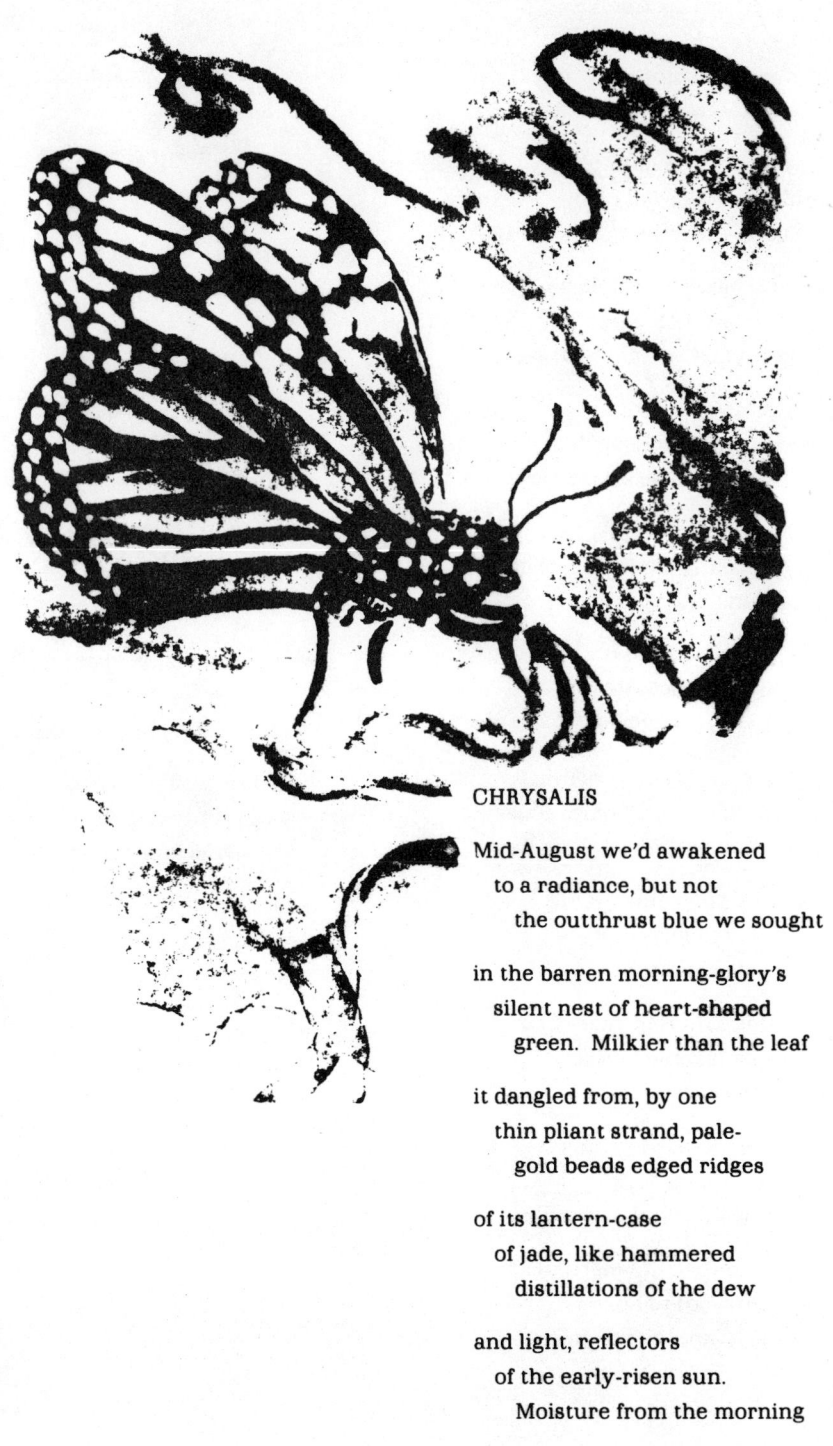

dripped from leaves
and clung, pooling
in circles of its faintly

terraced shell, its minute
orb of celadon,
that to the close eye

showed a pattern, even now—
pearl ghost of Monarch
wing—like an unformed

thought of something
yet to come. We watched
all day, in some odd sense

as if it were ourselves
transforming life we'd dreamt
to plan in hope

of change. And then
the night. Our flashlight
aimed, we watched

the waxen moisture breathe
and darken to the stained-glass
pattern of a russet wing.

At last, the morning edging
at the tips of trees
we shut the light

and slept, knowing once again
that life is rarely prisoned
by the ever-seeking

eye. Idea evades the limits
of the cupped flesh
of the hand. We'd risen

chastened that late morning
knowing not to hurry
down the stairs to grasp

the turning moment
of life's mysterious
change. But as we filled

our coffee cups and strolled
the porch-rail
to the trellised vine,

we knew already what
we'd see, and what
like last night's breathing

moisture, when our own
wings softly opened,
we would feel. And

it had emerged, its thought
complete, and ours
a little more so,

red-brown-black-sheen
pumping to a full sail
in the sun.

POPPIES

Sun dazzles the peach and orange
tremor of high **noon,**

the ever-so-slight waver
in the stillness that is air,

is earth—the legends
of narcosis settling

snow on lifted brows,
and fading altogether

in the broken spell of **dawn.**
Close petals flutter

as the breeze expands. Late noon.
Their stalks, sleek-furred,

lean criss-crossed
in keen shadows. This

is the evening, sun new-set,
to lie here, **still, among them,**

lambent in the afterglow,
a peach and orange palimpsest

of lost days, frail awakings.

REDWINGS, AGAIN

Irrational?—knowing I move
   through here every day,

strider down the river's
   snaking course, no egg-robbing

marauder of its young
   like the weed-sly mink

or thick-billed crow that daily try
   low nests wedged deep

in brush or built below
   the dust-dangle of sandbar willow

limbs, even beneath elderberry
   blooms, waist-high to a walker,

thatched bowls in the claw-sweep
   of stray cats. All summer

this strange terrified clown—
   shrill red on black—has shadowed

me, shrieking, leaping
   twig to twig, somersaulting

my bowed head, black knives
   quivering on the dusty path

I hurry down—blood-shock sudden
   in the light—then swoops

to waver, easy, bending
   weeds & grasses, hovering

on their utmost tips, yet never
   sinking quite to earth, a weightless

shimmering acrobat—then up
   again, his silhouette jet black

on the bright sun, like brief eclipse,
   to settle on the phone-pole

straight above me, demon-still.
   Epaulets, now folded, striped

a gentler yellow-red. But as I pass
   his hidden nest (somewhere

in the brush-line to my left?)
   he follows, still, to try new

stunts in the changed growth
   beyond the river's bend—calls

shriller now—to mark the final
   threat-range of the fierce

pulse of his mind. I *swear*
   I've seen him settle like a miracle

on tips—always the tips!—
   of mustard, timothy, wings

working just enough to balance
   there—metallic *chink* & piping

like the hot hiss of dry wind
   until my distance down the river's

winding path has clipped
   his rage. And then the vast

relief (for him, for me?) of sudden
   silence, cricket whir's soft pulse

in wide expanse of summer
   sun. Today, as riverbound,

I start out once again, thoughts
   only moments totally my own—

as almost always on these days
   before I turn the high-grassed

bend—I sense the hurtled
   shadow-shriek of his black burning

life above me now. And sometimes
   on these hot & restless nights

of mid-July, it hurtles nearer,
   shadowing false day—so near

on some, its burning shadow
   fuses with my own. But then

I wake. What's in his nest?
   Or do the tiny fledglings, grown

from their soft ashy fuzz,
   already stalk the aging

brush?—late July's brown
   kindling: dry timothy & Queen Anne's

lace—the thistles & the milkweed
   now grown high as watching

men, rough whispers in the wind.
   Some bright day, or in a wakeless

dream, he'll land, I know,
   will peck & peck, or talons

deep, at last, dissolve.

LUNA MOTH

Night-flyer, lovely as the swallowtail
yet hidden in pooled shadow

of the walnut grove—so rarely
seen—your soft & watery green

ascends again from the dark earth
where first you broke

your damp cocoon, ground-spun,
and rose to meet the summer moon,

bark-spread and luminous
for your brief life. An afterthought,

your slow ascent, pure & unstrained,
no mouth parts, only born

to breed (and only if a mate's scent
trickles by on the night breeze),

you force yourself on nothing
hunger artist of two weeks—only

to throb a limpid momentary
glow, as the green span of your wax

takes form, once more enters
my sleepless eyes, glazed memory,

more vivid now than the time
I saw you rise, but once,

in mid-July—sleepless under
nightwashed trees, & lingering.

Just like you, night-flyer,
stretched against the sable

bark (but softly stretched), damp dreamer,
green tails hanging with transparent

eyes, illusory but watchful
as pure vigilance, unforced

as inner thought, unheard,
yet lovely as the light-swept blue-black

swallowtail, bright suns gleaming
on its outstretched wings, as it flits

midday, from golden crowns
of sunflowers, to sway in plush-furred

gusts of thistle-pink. Not like you,
pure hidden one, stretched on bark & shadow

for two weeks. Night-flyer,
featherlike antennae spread

& sensitive to the night
breeze—rise from the dark earth

below my feet, brief stirrings,
before the flood of morning light,

to keep a soft green flame.

THE GERANIUM

   Pruned tidy in your
solid pot & placed against
   the summer sky
where I wash dishes

   even now, trained decoy
of your idleness, never
   seeming like pure
growth, yet subtler

   than artifice, you stand
always in middle-
   ground, your soft
round leaves' deceptive

   sleep, neat blooms'
still & delicate glow—a static
   force, like thought's
control, to break forth

   now in brilliant flame,
sprung loose in your
   collected blue, all symmetry
gone strange, askew,

   like the scream in the mouth
of a wild horse, mane
   spear-taut, keen scarlet tongue,
rushing forever through

   exterior wind.

FISHING AFTER RAIN

Pricked circlets gently loose
their silver scales into
lead depths. All's still.

We bend into the cushion
of wet air

around our heads, my boy & I,
legs dangling

from the chipped edge of sloped bridge
until our bobbers

all day still in the mud pond, though turned in wind,

begin, as one,
to lean & twitch, this instant

after rain—the earth-smells,
worm-scent,
sodden clothing's fumes

all suddenly
gone thick as brew we swallow
sensing bluegills,

bullheads wake to circle
now beneath our throbbing
legs,
    awakng now, as one,
in gathering light, at this strange hour
after rain,

the bobbers making firmer dips
& jerks. His goes down

fast, plump fingers
all a-clutch at the live line. My own's

plunged down in sudden swirl

but our sogged bait's lost cling
and's stolen quick. We

reel in lines, hooks bare,
the evening settling deep

as the clouds break. We pierce

new worms & cast out
one more time. Each feels a bite

like flash of sun. And
fast, I pull one
in. Again

his bait is gone. But he's
already tossed

his pole aside on the cement
and come to view my catch

with trembling
joy, like faith, renewed this hour
after rain,
        when the world's
changed from sleep to life, the bullhead
wriggling
black & thick, air upsucked
through whiskered
lips,
       gold eyes
needling deep into our own.

Unhook him now, red froth
on his left gill

but know his tough breed
destined still

to live, though bearing
ever after, one deep

scar. I let my glad boy
grasp his lower gut

and help me toss him back,
his glee & terror

fused, my gloved hand covering
the dorsal's

venomed spine. The pond
receives him

like dark lips, dim flick of tail,

he's gone. We now

sit still
a moment more, as one,
beneath low willows
like a darkening hut. Then
pack it up—
        hooks, sinkers,
bacon strips, the death-curled worms—

into our paper bag, walk back
to bikes, bush-chained,

in that sweet moisture
after rain, that bodied warmth
that made us know—
        a spirit
of the mud-dark air—

he'd rise.

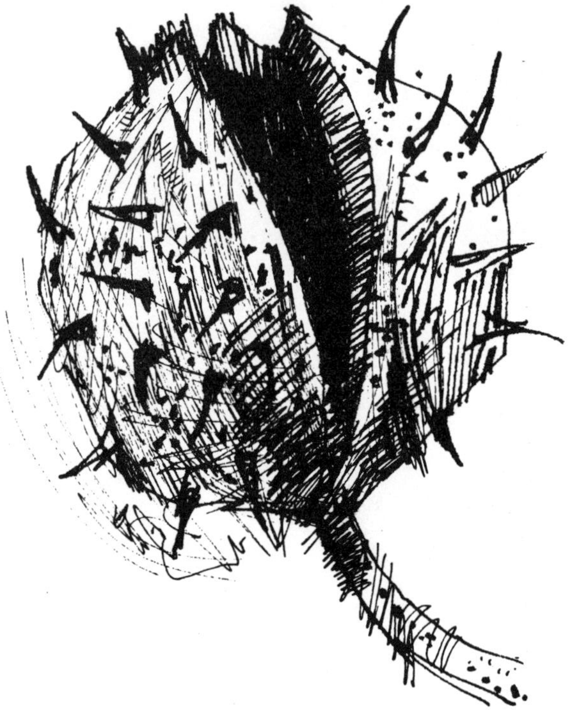

NUTGATHERERS

So the gentle couple down the street
    set out again

in early fall, across the bridge
    of the wooded

park, the mud flow rumbling
    underfoot, to squat

all day along the bank, their brown
    sacks open in bleached

grass, already strewn with
    the spiny husks,

wheels of coarse-toothed chestnut
    leaves, the craggy

bark behind them framing faces
    lifted pink in the crisp

wind, his hair shaggy as the rough
    leaves swept above,

her small face pinched tight in weathered
    blue, coatsleeves scraping

there, together, like tree-rustle
    as they pluck

the inedible fruit from waves & tufts
    of autumn grass.

There together, brown sacks open
    in the horsechestnuts'

great shadow, greeting neighbors—
    smiling gaily—

with raised chestnuts, as we pass.

SWALLOW EVENING

Stagnant puddle by the tracks. Swamp-
gloom. Residue in our small town

of two weeks' rain in early autumn's
sweep of musty brown. In marshscape

chill—our plain transformed—
they land & soar from branchfall

caught in mud. Those sodden
antlers rise upon this walker's

downturned eye.—The evening's
shaped by swallows, cream/brown

arrows skimming by my damp
& stiffened cheek, a small breeze

(I imagine?) swept behind, lifting
like warm light, each time,

this small-town walker's mind.
If not joy, I say to all

behaviorists, and to my doubting
self (bogged months & earthward

gaze), I know nothing of
the world—its quickened pulse

of energy turned love . . .

WINTER FEEDER BY THE WINDOW, FIRST OF DAWN

A flurry through the dull light
   like a quickened heart, the white breast
     of the nuthatch, snowbirds'

softer down, goldfinch faded
   to a gentler jewel of yellow/green
     have lifted, like a miracle,

my gaze that long ago stopped flitting
   limb to limb, on the old
     ailanthus' ruined hide—morning's

early visitant who leans like an awkward
   drunk along our pasteboard
     wall (old misfit tree, our

neighbors' grouse, I'd promised to remove
   this year, but for my wife's
     lament she'd nowhere else

to hang her shrine of winter
   charity)—the old ailanthus,
     circled by black seeds & crusts,

become, perhaps, our guardian
   against prejudice, clean septic things
     that nag at us within—pure

being clinging to the cracks—"clear faults"
   (our neighbors' well-meant words)
     along our unkempt wall—

wrinkles, whispered truths about
   our lives... But *they've*
     returned our offerings,

and more: their winter madrigal
   around our breadcrumbs, seeds,
     has lifted my sad head, eyes rising

    with the downy's crisp-veined
        back to peck the suet hammered
            to the grainy bark, and more. Lifted

    my sad head that long ago stopped flitting
        thought to thought. And now
            like a slow grand music, firmer

heart's no longer shocked by the sudden
    downthrust of a fragile limb
        in gust, the rise of fleeting

    wing (from brilliant gleam
        to sparrow brown), the ruby sting
            of the downy's startled flight. My eye's

grown firm against the ephemeral,
    the flux. My shadow at the window,
        winter mornings, first of dawn.

BEAVERS IN SNOW

Months now since we'd
seen their sleek backs
break the river's
slow flow toward the
east. To sound again
when sensing our still
presence on the bridge,
wakes sucked in bulging
hollows like the muscles
of their movement
on the water—branching
ripples cleaving to gold
chips, the sun's
last glow.
                Now
in the white season,
trees black runes
along the woodland's
silver edge, we stop
to view the relics
of their dark backs
bowed in tense & dogged
nerve work, never seen,
but in the warm
time, heard.
                We sense
their nearness beneath ice,
beneath the branch-logged
bend that marks the
river's turn, the half-sunk
mound, where backs hunch
in blind stillness, hunger
gnawing, briefly stir
to nibble twigs & bark, in trance,
they'd drawn to their nest's
opening, below.

            Gone,
the gust of willowood,
the August sun's
deep scent from new-gouged
bark, strewn chips
gleaming green & tan
that blazed another
nearness, summer's passion,
seen no longer circling
their season's epitaph
of leaning, sculptured
trunks, tomb-still, above
the dam that pressed
to a fine stream—
now glazed—the river's
bend.
            Tomb-still,
the leaning hourglass
forms, incisions like
pure code of left ideas
on their unfinished
curves, gouge-flecked
into the age-rings'
rippled flow—left now
for eyes of others
to complete. As if
to say, *work on, work
on*—the constant act
beyond acclaim, rough-hewn
tokens of a hard
task's joy. *Work on, work
on*—unfinished act. And then
the rare & perfect
scrape—pure accident—of eye
or brow, the tender curl,
that civilized the burly
cone, reminding
us of Brancusi
or Moore.

But as we walk
the last curve of the silver
maze toward home, life
in warm rooms—thoughts
softened by green leafspread
of the wallpaper's false
spring, tea cupped
like lovers' heads
lulled in the good thaw
of chill hands—those shapes
drift back, keen as before,
against the mind's
still white: The signs
of secret work, unsung,
bark-stripped & looming
there like truth. Or
perfect silent words.

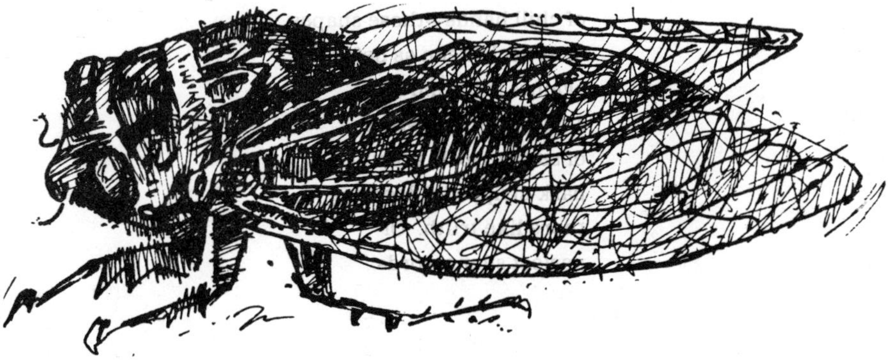

LIFE IN DEATH

I lift the dead cicada from his place
upon the sill—among tomatoes
in their last-picked ranks,
those soap-red mutants
of late fall, a vase
of drying dill. My wife's
still-life behind the sink—
distraction from my
rinsing, watch him start
to move along the hairfield
of my arm, above the rubber
glove, where I've placed
the weeklong stillness
of his solid black/green
hull—blunt head & vacant
bubbled eyes—to feel
the hooked hairs of his
feet, the tickle-prick
of death against my flesh,
confirming by its stillness
my full life?
                    And now the faint
vibrato, at first I'd thought
imagined, on my arm—a barely
deepening hum in his thick
corpse, torpid since the year's
first frost—etched in
ice-streaked glass
above us now. Death
I'd never doubted, despite
the rays of inlaid green
that glinted grass-fresh
through the wingthrust
down his black-bulked
flanks.

                    The faint buzz
tightens on my forearm, tiny
sway from side to side,
keen against the backdrop
of near death, the ice-
streaked window up above
merging flesh with shell
in dusky light, in silence
& clear cold: this breath
of life, vibrato, edging down
my forearm, dazzlingly firm
in its faint pull, clarity of torpor's
hidden spark: much too vast
(& close) for us to
grasp in the world's
energetic haste.

STILL LIFE

Below the wild parsnip, dried in umbelled reach—forever,
Dull and tawny gold, the husk of the cicada
Bows, forever, like a seer crouched, amazed bubbles
Of chitin peering out like amber globes. The vision,
Seen forever, is the soft translucent
Glimmer of a sparrow's weathered skull—its cranium,
A perfect egg, throws back a tiny light
Toward the open casement, setting sun's
Pale glow. Flecked in minute
Shadowed pores, the brittle lower beak
Has come unhinged, lies between
The opal skull and hunched cicada . . .

                    It is the jeweled grain
Of the red-ear's burnished carapace
That backs them like a hillock
Where the fragment of a Roman pot—the fractured
Lip—lies lofty in grey shadow: figment
Of the ruin of St. Albans. Time creeps on.
2,000 years. A grey ceramic. Dust.
Air's caressing rub will merge these things . . .
                      Slow dust between
The clay, shell, flesh, the weed and bone,
Forever.

HUMAN NATURE

It must be borne in mind that my design is not to write histories but lives... Sometimes a matter of less moment, an expression or jest, informs us better of men's characters and inclinations than the most glorious expolits. Therefore, as portrait-painters are more exact in the lines and features of the face, in which the character is seen, than in the other parts of the body, so I must be allowed to give my more particular attention to the marks and indications of the souls of men, and while I endeavor by these to portray their lives, may be free to leave more weighty matters ... to be treated by others.

—Plutarch, *Lives*

BATS

We called them bats.
Backstreets of Chicago,
evening wind,
the howls began.
School weathered, odd jobs
punched & supper
down, they'd flock
the alley hoops
beneath our blackened
walls of brick, knowing
to a stroke, in almost-dark,
when brother bats
would come—just time
to shoot for teams
before the alley roofs
were gone. And then
the howls began, till midnight
never ceased on those hot summers
in Chicago, hovered
rising, falling
in that city's constant
wind.
        Evenings
out to grab a bite
or come home late
to mount the wooden stairs
that climbed the backs
of our brick flats
like chipped white trellises
into the fortressed
heights, we'd glimpse them
under streetlights, dark wind
whistling,
        a music
like all-knowing, somehow wonderful
& strange,

     high fingers spread
& vanishing in the last streaks
of red sky,
     dim forms
floating, weaving
in those patterns not rehearsed
yet always smooth,
      spurred
by howls & muffled
hoots & never
to be quite the same
again,
    until—still hush—
a perfect roll
off fingers, the ball's rise
in the pooled glow,
the deep swish of assent
(that never seen), slapped hands,
the music stopped . . .

Blind as bats
in the alleys of Chicago.
No longer dazzled
by the day's bright web
of words. They played
by feel & that's
how they got good.

THE BEAUTIFUL FACE

What aching when we
see it—flash in restaurant
glance above the menu's
plastic glare (we know
to never look again);
passing stranger on
a bus, white knuckles
gripping tight to the steel
rings & quickly
by (swift intimacy
not our own); or storm evacuee
on the TV from some
flood-buried Midwest town,
its name & Main Street
echoing our own (but not
our own); or herded
in old footage from the
Holocaust, brown eyes
luminous as moons
beneath the knit waves
of black brows—long dead,
we know, but charged
with passion in the instant's
heart-pumped air—or, now,
this very face before
me, getting off the Greyhound,
suitcase clasped forever
in the station's
giddy blur, & swirling
from the warm clasp
of my heart.

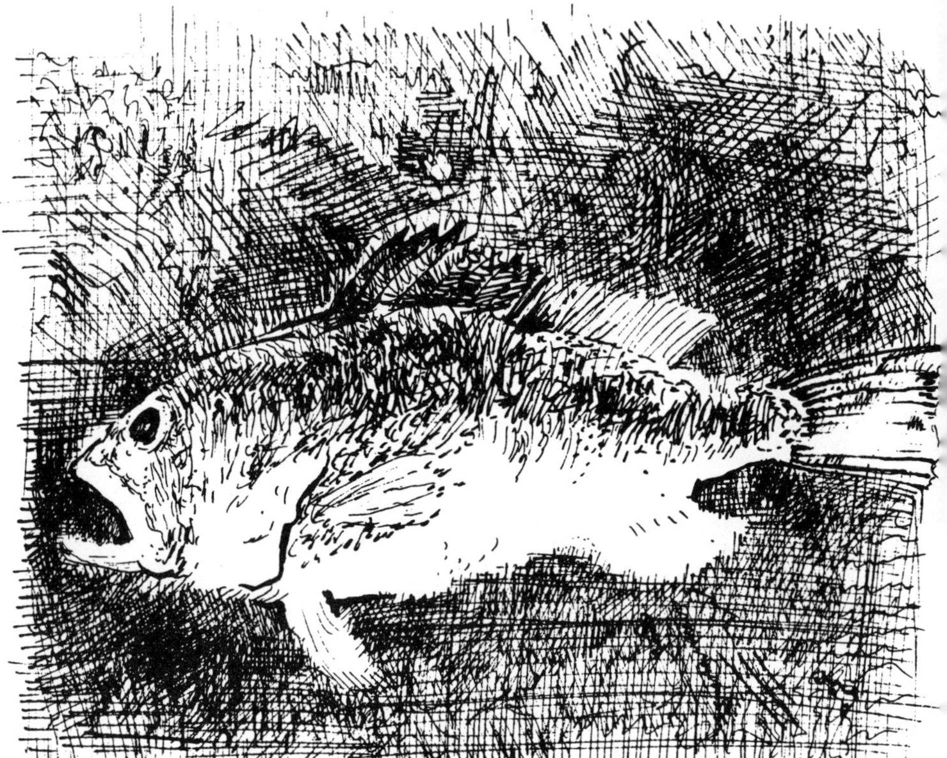

ON TAKING MY OLD FATHER TO THE CHICAGO AQUARIUM

Idling at a red, I glance along the dashboard
to my father: stockingcap, head bobbing

like a hawk's, the asphalt's rising heat
sapped in the hollow of his jaw. He murmurs.

I'm not sure, but give him gum, thrust into
the Lake Shore drone again. Later, by the

tanks, he's still bound north—eyes
glazed past the spinning pike, the shark,

the loggerheads hung silvered in their nostril-
cleaving bursts. I press his arm, its sinew

tough as horn: he nods, regards the fanning
pectorals, grins at tapered snouts. A grouper,

dazed, has met him eye to eye. It looks away.
We pass into the smaller worlds, the angels,

sunfish pause, slough bubbles, dart lit kelp.
Their vibrant chaos swarms his eyes with tears.

He turns and yawns. Away, we trace late glimmer
of the lake-waves frothing sands. I point. He's fast

asleep, a boy's wry smile craggy on a rock I've
scanned and scanned. I look back to the shore-

line, now grown dim, feel the cool tide
riffling shallows, sense the soundless gaze of fish.

ANTIQUE

Alive or dead, we never knew.

The telephone book just sat there
where the boy from Bell
had tossed it, ducking rain.

It was well known the old man
had no phone.

Dim and constant through the transom
one bare lightbulb
stirred the neighbors
like a pulse.

Not quite tossed beneath the canopy
above his bowing stoop, it rotted there
in sun, wind, rain, became
a core of wood, a marking post
for feral cats, a urinal for dogs. . . .

SAINTS OF SPRING

As I walk each night
beneath the shrouding sycamores,

the grey-green camouflage
of molting skins, I cannot stop my eyes

from drifting like a thief's
into the glowing living rooms

where the weak-eyed elders
sit among the photographs

of sons long gone, smiles
lit pink, or one, alone,

clear-eyed in olive uniform,
cap's tilt a little rakish

toward the crisp tip
of his ear; the girls, in school,

all mothers now, coifed there
forever like the glossy backs

of mink, white teeth
set firm.
         They shadow
boards of solitaire or evening news

read yet again, felt visors down
beneath bright lamps, casting

a soft green pall over their faces,
flowing out—eyes glittering—

into the frigid air
 turning to spring.

PORCH

Biking home under
streetlights
from the local gym,
street shadows full,
a slight wind
in the trees.
          No bikelight
still. I love these streets
this hour—their intimate
evening dark, and will risk
webs & ruts
to ride unseen.

          She's out again
as I near home, grease-heavy hair
reflecting light
& hanging forward
on her young/old head.

The brood around her
on the wood porch
clings—
      a new one, howling,
lumped upon the steps,
gripping at the glazed ropes
of her hair.

          Shadows
from a large oak
cross her back, the nape
& spine still delicate
in the dark.
          Warm gold light
behind her, through the kitchen's
open door
          circles her bowed
          silhouette
          like a saint's,

the children, small dim devils,
dream-tormentors,
snapping round.

Perhaps to last's enough:
bear mother-woes.
She grips the railing
as the nighttime
falls.

THE SAD AND NOBLE POEMS
OF THE ANCIENT CHINESE CONCUBINES

Always the tone is weary,
resolute—the fading eyes,
thin wrinkles spreading
like the ripples of the Yangtze
into evening mist. The distant moon

hollow and cold. And then the notes
heard from the castle's
heights, the accompanying voice
no longer hers, no longer
warm. Distances

deceive, yet what in
life, warm, sweet,
is not deception? This she's gained.
She lifts her silk sleeve
to her brow, blackening

the moonbeams' slanted brace
of quiet. On this chill night
again, she thinks of
him, his laughter,
practiced charm, her own

small face, pure ivory,
which then and now
was bound to last
forever, he had told her,
where she was.

LYNN

Third time severed—this time
from a drunk who'd beat her silly
with the very shovel that she'd

tilled the garden with—its always
rich & florid growth—till her teenaged
daughter'd called the cops & got him

nailed. They'd warned she dare not
stick it out, or if she did
the thing was odds to be born

witless, blue, or worse. "She'd
best abort." But never Lynn
to go the easy way for this

or anything—quick promised needle-
puff of air, the aftermath of
anesthetic calm. And we all watched

in wonder, as hauled away from
swabbing at the nearby factory
floor, this janitress, destined for life

to be mostly alone—we knew it
then & know it now—bore Amy, effortlessly
they   said, whole & lovely as a china

doll—her sagging body's second
perfect pearl.

SMOKE

Pedaling home from evening work
down autumn streets, the neighborhood
I've roamed for years, from yard-creeper to

now, this instant, blazed
to special foreignness—leaf-fires
both dizzying and crisp,

like watchful and yet dreaming eyes
through the smoke-edged limbs
of scant-leaved trees—the world

a shifting greyish blue, my heart
rapping like wood against my ribs
as I breathe in and out

with each leg's thrust.
The time has come again—my boy,
fat-cheeked, will sing me

birthday songs before the fireplace
tonight, his mother's arranged act.
I love them both. I'm tired

but alive. The darkness
falls before I reach
my home, touch them with the music

of the garage door's slow creak.

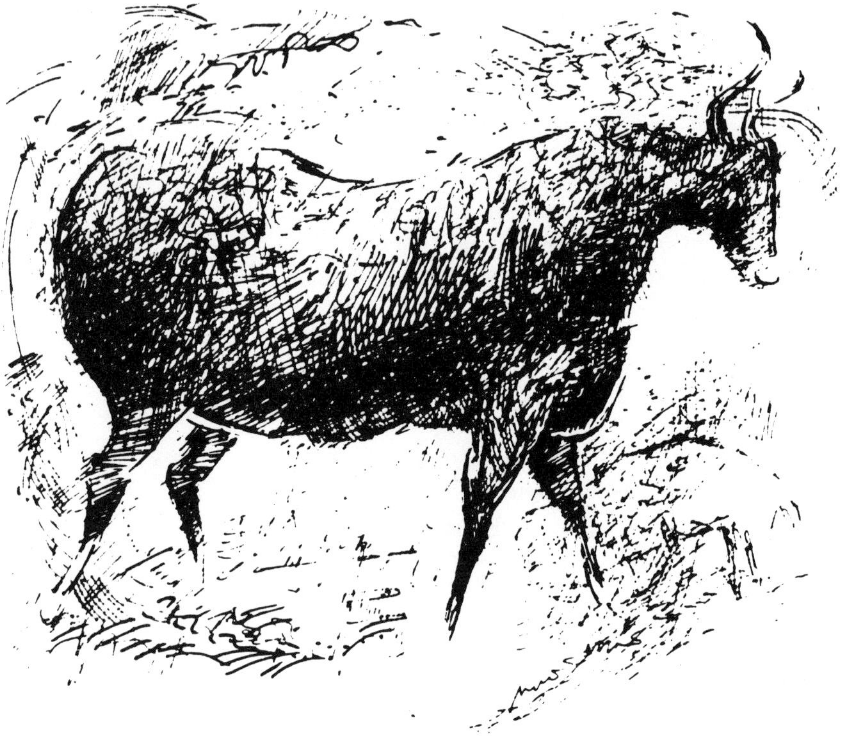

CAVE BULL

My wife's quick
   drawing thrills the children
     at our youngster's

school. Later, parent's
   duty done—their monthly
     lesson on Lascaux—

its brown massy shag's
   been hung: a "vision"
     on our bathroom

wall—the delicate swirl
   of hoof & horn, scratched
     fur, the nostril's

terrible curl. A small deer
   lifts his soft-red snout
     to whistle from

the distance. I start.
   Grown cool, the bathwater's
     a waterhole from where

I now return (boy out
   to play, wife tame
     about our evening

meal). Sly, certain
   that there's no one
     near, I wade

back out, bent ripple-low,
   fist tightening round
     my trembling spear.

LEMONADE STAND
(But for This Knowledge There Is Time)

My small son & the neighbor
kids sit all day
    beneath the burning

sun with the 10¢-
sign I'd scrawled
    them on a board.

No traffic stops. No
shadows pass. The dream
    of piled dimes

has worn to sweaty
brows & tears. Strategically,
    before they break,

before the world sags
down with too much
    truth, my wife & I

stroll out, bright quarters
held aloft in the noonday
    glare. Like grateful

patrons, overspend: thanking
them—those gleeful sweaty
    faces the world won't.

But for this knowledge
    there is time.

PUSH-MOWER

Tell my neighbor, his
cranked motor running
    (*Want to use it when*

I'm through?)—"No,
really, I prefer
    mine, Bernie; it's

what makes me tough."
(I remind him
    how on good days

I can stay with
him, in one-on-one,
    though old enough

to be his dad.) I
cannot tell him
    that it's actually

my love of silence,
time alone & cricket
    song—the only

cure I know for
"writer's block." The muscles
    blent, as Whitman

mused, with the heady
    flow of grass.

BEGINNERS' LUCK

Dips it in—an awkward
motion off the pier—
   is screaming for me,

just like that, to help
him pull it up: a 4-lb.
   carp! Now untangling

his leg, I watch
out of the corner
   of my eye, the old-timer

who's always there
& gives up tips—(his
   two lines out

even in rain)—stand
above my youngster's
   gasping gold-finned

prize, & gawk. "Damn
goofy kid"—his jealous
   loving rasp (sounds of

too much smoke & beer,
of life's denials, things
   unhooked)—yet

hands my kid his only
heavy stringer—the one's
   held all his luck—"So

the kid can take
him home." We thank
   him, my thoughts

as we pedal back (the glad
boy mounted there
   behind me, like

an emperor, on his yellow
child's throne) are of shed
   years, pure nonchalance

&, yes, beginners' luck.

SQUIRREL ELECTROCUTED ON THE POWER LINE

It dangles like a martyr
   cheeks more gaunt each day
in the shrill Virginia
   sun of late September.
And each day it troubles
   me, troubles me a little
more, as I walk beneath it
   with my son, each day
a little more, until its dried
   & dangling paws outstretched
in loss beneath thin line-
   glued feet, the patched
& matted fur gone now
   from fawn to grey
have troubled us enough
   to cause us to divert
our daily walk, to take
   the long way up the ruby-
yellow hills where squirrels
   leap & climb as we move
past, untroubled now,
   untroubled as the setting
sun behind the dimming
   hills of late September.

THE SKUNK

For weeks, each night
we know his snout

in trash: the faint but acrid
scent of his slight

fear (breeze-borne trickle
of his ready spray).

Each night, each sultry
summer night,

his black/white waddle
roots about our

sleeping waking dreams—
reminds us sharply

nothing living's isolate
or clean. And in the morning,

carnage of damp shreds
and scattered cans.

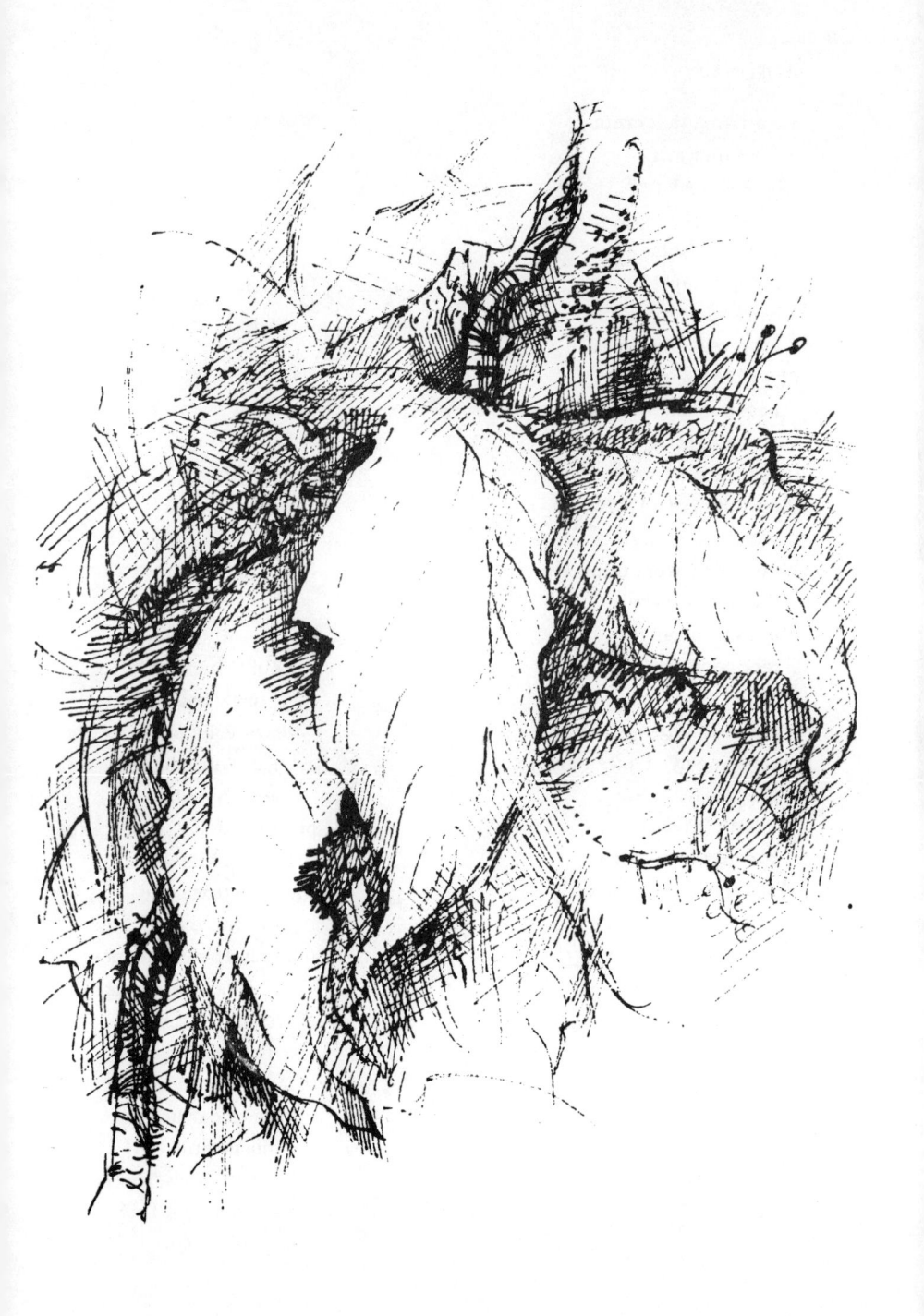

POISON IVY

Slow flame that crept
   my inner arm
(the way its hairy-
   rooted vine crawled
up the oak's thick
   bole)—that left
a scarlet berry-patch,
   brighter than the rose
tips of its dangling
   hump-lobed leaves—
then blossomed down
   my back & thighs.
First token of a Virginia
   woods—my first
home away from Illinois—
   that left a rash
like some strange
   leprosy four days
of drugs & steaming
   baths could barely
cleanse away. I'd thought
   the trip from North
to South (in early fall),
   the myth of a shed
skin ("to start again")

would change my
luck, draw back spent
   years, & let me
start, a "Southerner,"
   anew. Avoid, like
plague, the harsh mistakes
   of old. I knew not
then the toxic oily
   glow, three dangling
tongues, the vengeance
   of this hidden "snake
of weeds." But along
   with many signs
of late—red stippled glow
   in the clear light—
I'm mortal still, I'm
   marked again (there's
little change), & I
   accept my fate.

ABOUT THE AUTHOR

Dan Stryk is the author of two previous collections of poetry, *To Make a Life* (Confluence Press) and *The Artist and the Crow* (Purdue University Press). His poems appear regularly in a variety of national publications, including *TriQuarterly, Commonweal, Poetry Northwest, Western Humanities Review,* and *The Hollins Critic.* Dan Stryk has also been the recipient of a number of state and national literary awards, including an Illinois Arts Council Poetry Grant, and a National Endowment for the Arts Poetry Fellowship. After spending much of his life in the Midwestern heartland of Illinois, the poet now lives in Bristol, Virginia, with his wife, the artist Suzanne Stryk, and his son, Theo. He is currently an Associate Professor of World Literature and Creative Writing at Virginia Intermont College.